T0401142

APOLLO

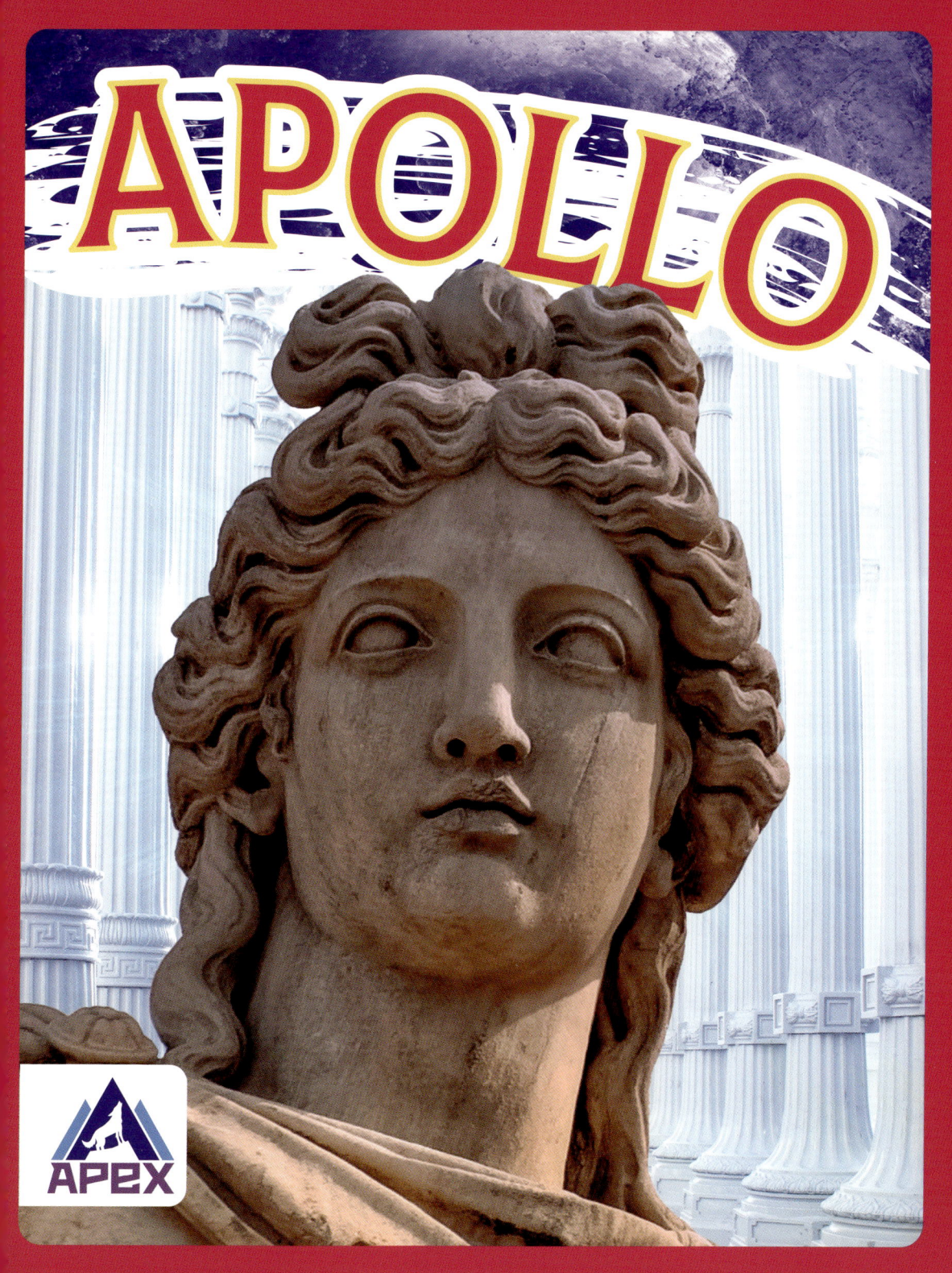

BY CHRISTINE HA

WWW.APEXEDITIONS.COM

Apex is distributed by North Star Editions:
sales@northstareditions.com | 888-417-0195

Produced for Apex by Red Line Editorial.

Photographs ©: Shutterstock Images, cover, 1, 4–5, 6, 7, 8–9, 10–11, 12–13, 14–15, 18, 22–23, 24–25, 26, 26–27, 29; iStockphoto, 16–17, 19, 20–21

Library of Congress Control Number: 2020952911

ISBN
978-1-63738-011-6 (hardcover)
978-1-63738-047-5 (paperback)
978-1-63738-117-5 (ebook pdf)
978-1-63738-083-3 (hosted ebook)

Printed in the United States of America
Mankato, MN
082021

NOTE TO PARENTS AND EDUCATORS

Apex books are designed to build literacy skills in striving readers. Exciting, high-interest content attracts and holds readers' attention. The text is carefully leveled to allow students to achieve success quickly. Additional features, such as bolded glossary words for difficult terms, help build comprehension.

TABLE OF CONTENTS

CHAPTER 1

THE GOLDEN SUN

A woman woke up very early. The sky was still dark. But morning was coming. A god flew just above the **horizon**. It was Apollo.

Apollo was a major Greek god. Light was one of many things he controlled.

Fiery horses pulled Apollo's golden **chariot**. Flames trailed behind him. He was pulling the sun across the sky.

A carving of Apollo's chariot can be found on a theater in Milan, Italy.

The goddess Artemis protected girls and young women.

APOLLO'S TWIN

Apollo had a twin sister named Artemis. She was the goddess of the moon and hunting. She rode her own chariot across the sky. It brought night.

Apollo (center) and Artemis (right) were the children of Leto (left) and the god Zeus.

Apollo soared higher and higher. The sky grew lighter as he went. Day had begun.

In early Greek stories, Helios was the god of the sun. But people combined Helios and Apollo into one figure over time.

CHAPTER 2

MANY POWERS

Apollo was best known as the god of the sun. But he also had power over art, music, **prophecy**, medicine, and **archery**.

Apollo was one of the few gods who had the same name in both Greek and Roman myths.

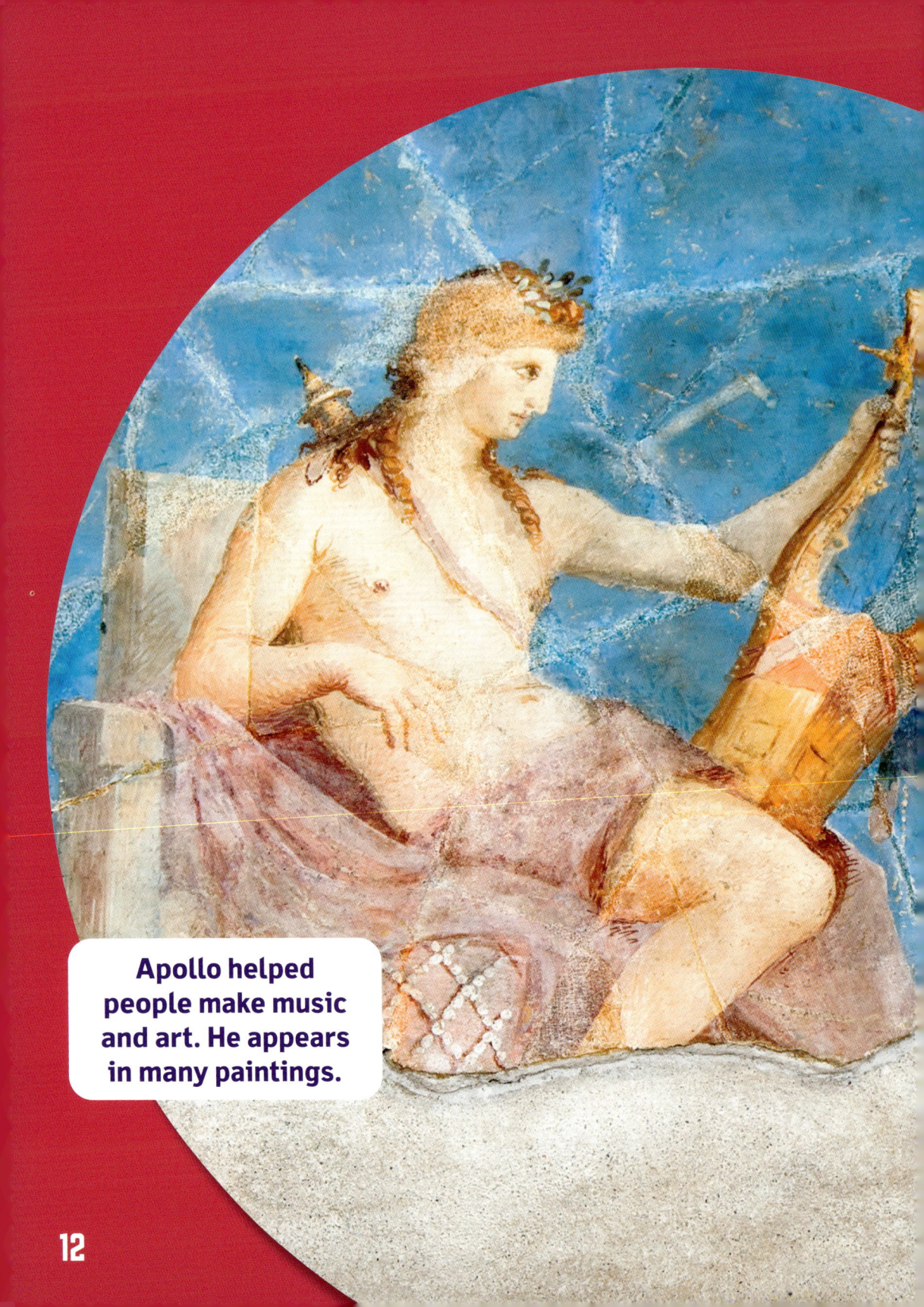

Apollo helped people make music and art. He appears in many paintings.

Apollo was a god of justice, law, and order. He helped people have peace and safety. He also watched over governments and cities.

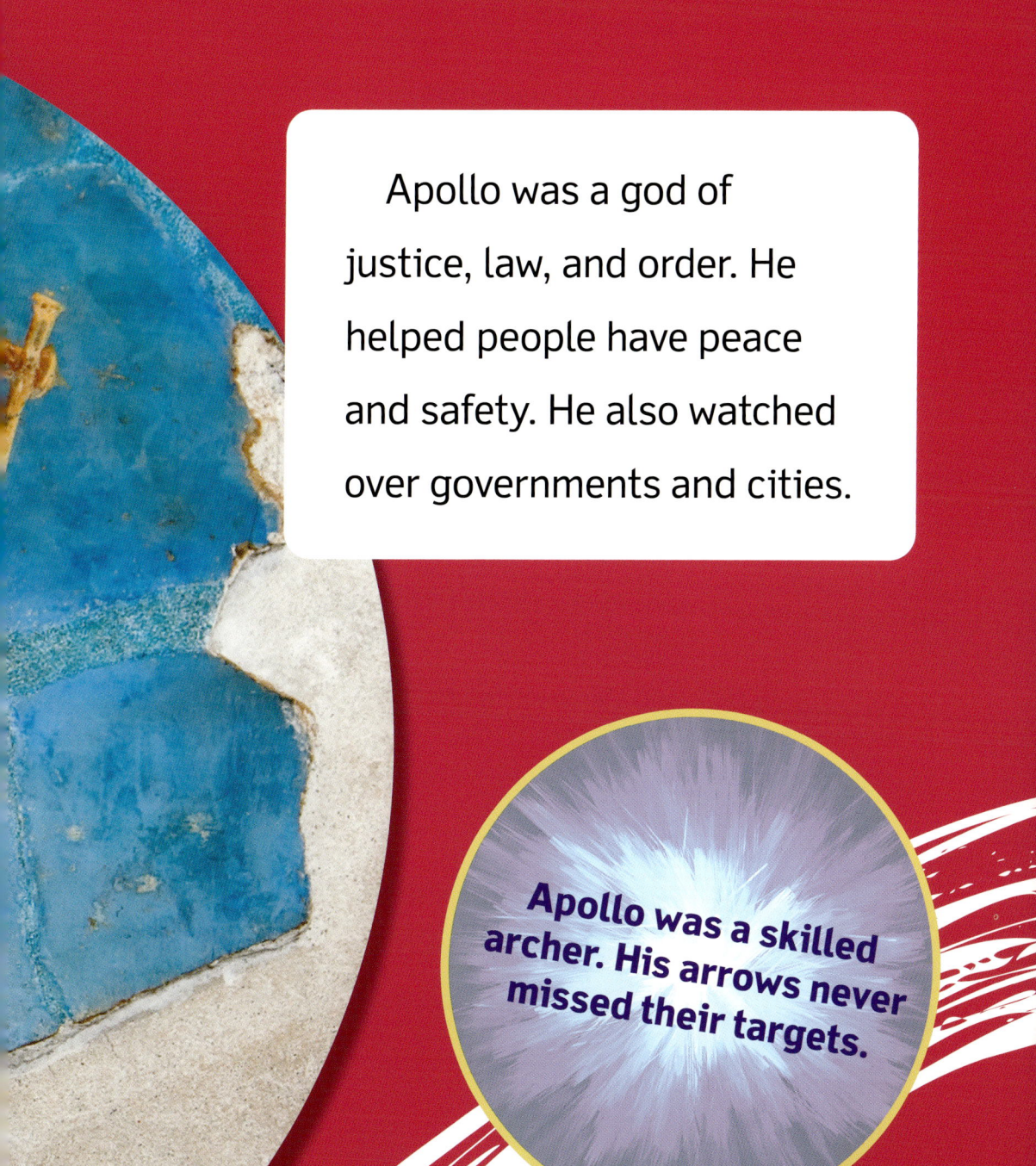

Apollo was a skilled archer. His arrows never missed their targets.

Apollo got his lyre from the god Hermes.

Apollo played a **lyre**. This instrument made beautiful music. It also had magical powers. It could **charm** people.

PROUD MUSICIAN

Once, Apollo and the god Pan had a music contest. Apollo won. But one listener thought Pan was better. Apollo got angry. He cursed that man by giving him donkey ears.

CHAPTER 3

UNLUCKY IN LOVE

Apollo was described as young and handsome. He fell in love often. But it usually ended badly. Many of his lovers died suddenly.

One person Apollo loved was a prince from Sparta. Legends say blue flowers grew where the prince died.

The god Eros made Apollo (right) fall in love with Daphne (left). Then he made Daphne run from Apollo.

Apollo loved Daphne. She was turned into a laurel tree. Its leaves became a symbol of Apollo.

Other people didn't love him back. Apollo did not like being rejected. He sometimes punished these people.

Apollo is often shown wearing a crown of laurel leaves.

For example, Apollo loved Cassandra. He taught her prophecy. But she did not love him. So, he cursed her. After that, no one believed what she **predicted**.

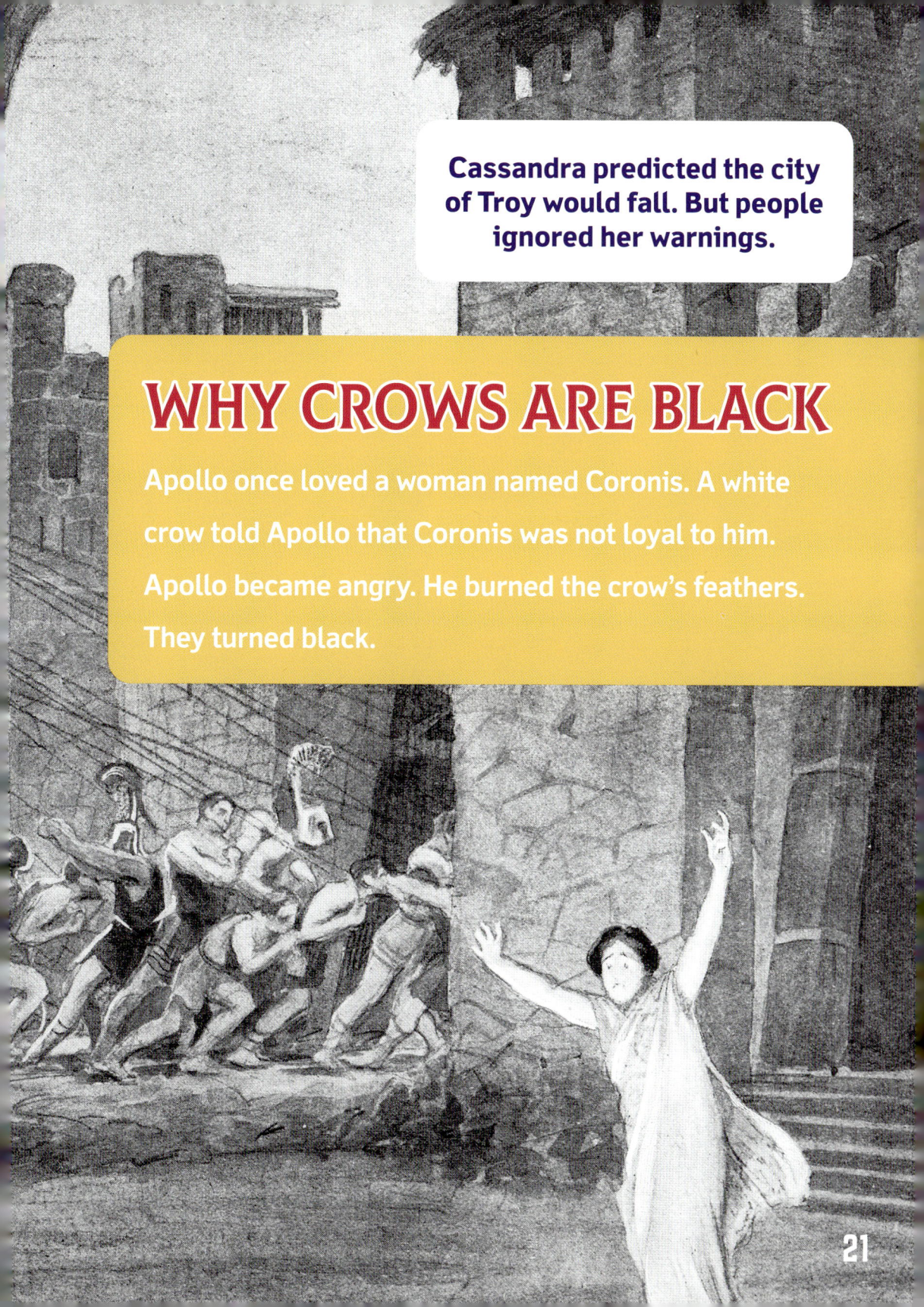

Cassandra predicted the city of Troy would fall. But people ignored her warnings.

WHY CROWS ARE BLACK

Apollo once loved a woman named Coronis. A white crow told Apollo that Coronis was not loyal to him. Apollo became angry. He burned the crow's feathers. They turned black.

CHAPTER 4

APOLLO'S TEMPLE

The Greeks built many temples for Apollo. The most important temple was in the city of Delphi. This temple had a famous **oracle**.

Ruins of the Temple of Apollo at Delphi still stand today.

A treasury held the gifts people brought to the oracle.

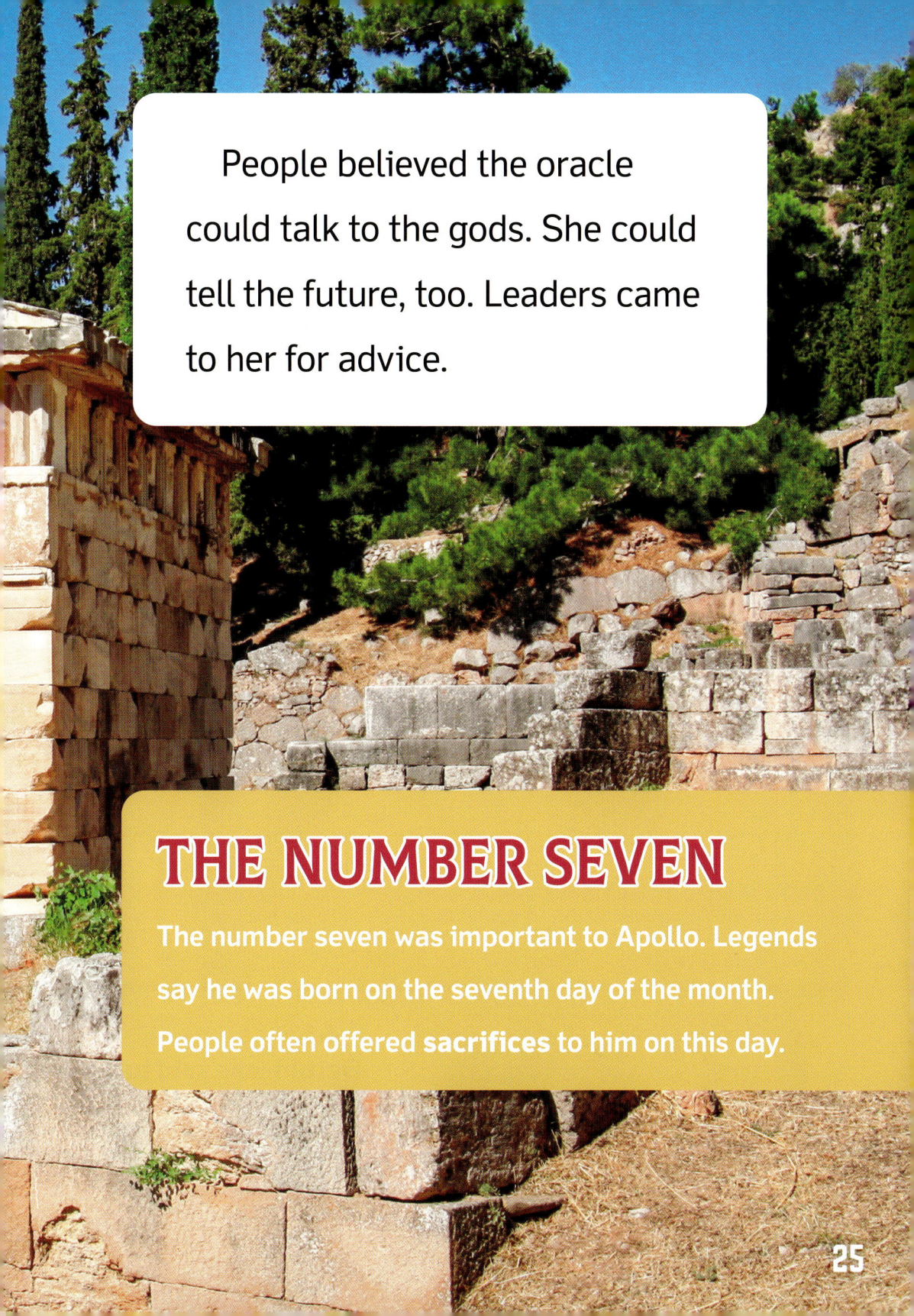

People believed the oracle could talk to the gods. She could tell the future, too. Leaders came to her for advice.

THE NUMBER SEVEN

The number seven was important to Apollo. Legends say he was born on the seventh day of the month. People often offered **sacrifices** to him on this day.

The temple stood on a mountain. It was hard to get to. But people came from all over. They brought laurel branches, money, and sacrifices. In return, they got advice.

A holy stone at Delphi was said to mark the center of the world.

A statue of Apollo guards the ruins of a temple in Italy.

Apollo had temples outside Greece, too. Some were as far away as Egypt and Turkey.

COMPREHENSION QUESTIONS

Write your answers on a separate piece of paper.

1. Write a few sentences explaining the main ideas of Chapter 3.

2. Would you want to have someone predict your future? Why or why not?

3. Where was the most important temple of Apollo located?

    A. Egypt
    B. Delphi
    C. Turkey

4. Why would people bring laurel branches to Apollo's temple?

    A. Laurel trees were very expensive.
    B. Laurel trees were not important.
    C. Laurel trees were a symbol of Apollo.

5. What does **rejected** mean in this book?

*Other people didn't love him back. Apollo did not like being **rejected**.*

   A. prayed to
   B. followed around
   C. not loved or wanted

6. What does **cursed** mean in this book?

*Apollo got angry. He **cursed** that man by giving him donkey ears.*

   A. made friends with someone
   B. hurt someone with magic
   C. was kind to someone

Answer key on page 32.

GLOSSARY

archery
The skill of shooting arrows with a bow.

chariot
A two-wheeled cart pulled by horses or other animals.

charm
To use magic to control someone or something.

horizon
The place where the ground and the sky seem to meet.

lyre
A stringed instrument that is similar to a small harp.

oracle
A person who tells messages to and from the gods.

predicted
Said that something will happen in the future.

prophecy
The ability to predict the future.

sacrifices
Gifts to gods or goddesses to win their help or favor.

symbol
An object or idea that stands for and reminds people of something else.

TO LEARN MORE

BOOKS

Bell, Samantha S. *Ancient Greece*. Lake Elmo, MN: Focus Readers, 2020.

Flynn, Sarah Wassner. *Greek Mythology*. Washington, DC: National Geographic, 2018.

Temple, Teri. *Apollo: God of the Sun, Healing, Music, and Poetry*. Mankato, MN: The Child's World, 2019.

ONLINE RESOURCES

Visit **www.apexeditions.com** to find links and resources related to this title.

ABOUT THE AUTHOR

Christine Ha lives in Minnesota. She enjoys reading and learning about myths and legends from around the world.

INDEX

Answer Key:
1. Answers will vary; **2.** Answers will vary; **3.** B; **4.** C; **5.** C; **6.** B